Joh

ALASKA

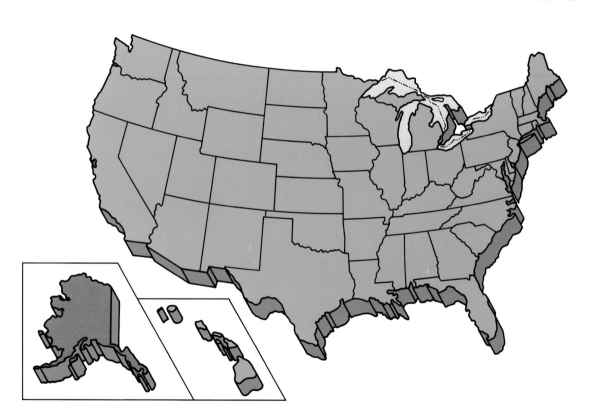

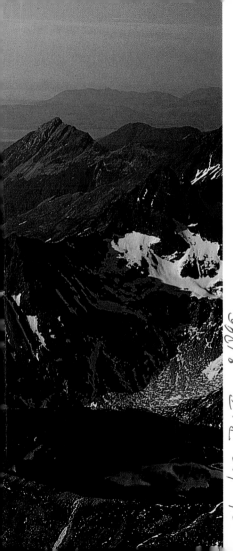

ALASKA

Joyce Johnston

Lerner Publications Company

LIBRARY OF CONGRESS
CATALOGING-IN-PUBLICATION DATA
Johnston, Joyce.
    Alaska / Joyce Johnston
      p. cm. — (Hello USA)
    Includes bibliographical references and index.
    Summary: Introduces the geography, history, people, industries, and environmental concerns of the Last Frontier.
    ISBN 0-8225-2735-9 (lib. bdg.)
    1. Alaska—Juvenile literature. 2. Alaska—Geography—Juvenile literature. [1. Alaska.] I. Title. II. Series.
F904.3.J64 1994
979.8—dc20   93-25401
                        CIP
                        AC

Manufactured in the United States of America

1 2 3 4 5 6 – I/JR – 99 98 97 96 95 94

Cover photograph by Lynn M. Stone.

The glossary that begins on page 68 gives definitions of words shown in **bold type** in the text.

CONTENTS

Did You Know . . . ?

❏ Although Alaskan summers are short, the sun shines about 20 hours each day and helps to produce enormous vegetables. Cabbages, for example, can grow to be as heavy as 80 pounds (36 kilograms)!

❏ Alaska's yearly catch of fish is larger and worth more money than the catch of any other state in the nation.

❏ Every year, more bald eagles flock to southeastern Alaska than to any other spot in the world. The fish-eating birds are attracted by easy-to-catch salmon that are swimming upriver.

❏ Alaska has more than 100,000 **glaciers**. One of these large masses of packed ice and snow, Malaspina Glacier, is North America's biggest glacier. It is larger than the state of Rhode Island.

❏ The world's longest chain of active volcanoes is in Alaska. Since the year 1700, at least 41 different volcanoes have erupted in Alaska. Some of them have blown up as many as 25 times.

Passengers on a ship get a close-up view of one of Alaska's many glaciers.

Puffs of cotton sedge flutter in the sun.

A Trip Around the State

"Mush!" That's what some dogsled drivers yell to start their dog teams down a snow-covered trail. Because Alaska is as far north as you can go and still be in the United States, you might think that the state is nothing but endless snowy trails in a land of ice and cold. But Alaska is also a land of rain and fog, mighty mountains, steaming volcanoes, and colorful plants and animals.

Alaska is the largest state in the United States. More than twice the size of Texas, Alaska is known for its vast wilderness. The state has almost 200 national and state parks, forests, and other areas protected by the government.

Every year, Alaska's fur seals travel thousands of miles south to spend the winter in the warm waters along the coast of Mexico.

Like the island state of Hawaii, Alaska is not physically connected to the rest of the United States. The Pacific Ocean, the Canadian province of British Columbia, and Canada's Yukon Territory separate Alaska from the 48 mainland states. Alaskans call the mainland states the Lower 48.

Water forms most of Alaska's borders. The Gulf of Alaska and the stormy Pacific Ocean lie south of the state. To the west are the Bering Sea and the narrow Bering Strait. North of Alaska is the icy Arctic Ocean. These bodies of water are home to whales, fish such as salmon and halibut, and many types of shellfish. Sea otters, fur seals, and many seabirds live along the coasts.

10

ARCTIC OCEAN

RUSSIA

Prudhoe Bay

NORTHWEST TERRITORIES

RUSSIA

UNITED STATES

ARCTIC COASTAL PLAIN

Colville River

BROOKS RANGE

Bering Strait

Porcupine River

CANADA

UNITED STATES

St. Lawrence Island

Nome

UPLANDS AND LOWLANDS

Yukon River

Fairbanks

Tanana River

YUKON TERRITORY

ALASKA

Regional boundary
International boundary

Miles
0   10   20   30   40   50

Kilometers
0 10 20 30 40 50

N

▲ *Mt. McKinley*

PACIFIC MOUNTAINS

Kuskokwim River

Anchorage

Valdez

Prince William Sound

Malaspina Glacier

JUNEAU ★

BRITISH COLUMBIA

Bering Sea

Sitka

Kodiak Island

Gulf of Alaska

Ketchikan

Islands

Alaska Peninsula

PACIFIC OCEAN

Alaska has four land regions. They are stacked on top of one another from south to north. The Pacific Mountains make up the southernmost region, topped by the Uplands and Lowlands region, the Brooks Range, and the Arctic Coastal Plain. Altogether, Alaska's four regions are shaped like a square kite with two tails.

The two tails are part of the Pacific Mountain region. One tail drifts west into the ocean from Alaska's southwestern corner. It includes a **peninsula** called the Alaska Peninsula and a chain of

The rivers and lakes of the Alaska Peninsula are famous for the many fish they contain.

American Indians named Mount McKinley *Denali*, which means "great one" or "high one." The huge mountain is so rugged that only about half of the mountaineers who have climbed it have actually reached the top.

islands called the Aleutian Islands. The other tail drops from Alaska's southeastern corner. Made up of islands and a narrow strip of coast, this tail is known as the Alaska Panhandle.

Many rugged mountain chains wrinkle the landscape in the Pacific Mountain region. These ranges are part of the Coast Ranges—a mountain system that extends down the Pacific coast of North America as far as southern California. One of Alaska's peaks, Mount McKinley, pokes through the clouds at 20,320 feet (6,194 meters)—higher than any other mountain in North America. Large white sheep called Dall sheep climb the hillsides of the Pacific Mountains.

The biggest region in Alaska is the Uplands and Lowlands. Low hills separate the region's wide, swampy river valleys. Alaska's longest river, the muddy Yukon, winds all the way across this region, from the Yukon Territory in Canada to the Bering Sea. Several of Alaska's other major rivers—including the Kuskokwim, Tanana, and Porcupine—also flow through the Uplands and Lowlands region.

The area around the Yukon River is home to reindeer and musk-ox. About 80 percent of the world's emperor and Canada geese nest there in the summer.

Alaska's Brooks Range is the northernmost arm of the Rocky Mountains, a chain that extends southward through Canada and the Lower 48 as far as New Mexico. The Brooks Range is Alaska's most untamed land region, and few people live here. Caribou, moose, wolves, porcupines, and grizzly bears roam through the region's wildlife preserves and wilderness areas.

A strip of land that has been cleared of trees marks a section of the border between Alaska and Canada.

Wildlife in the Brooks Range
includes grizzly bears *(left)* and gray
wolves *(below)*.

The flat Arctic Coastal Plain lies north of the Brooks Range. Also called the North Slope, the plain gradually drops from the foothills of the Brooks Range to the Arctic Ocean. Only the top few inches of soil on the Arctic Coastal Plain thaw in the summer. Because the soil below is always frozen, the ground is called **permafrost**. The

Because permafrost is always frozen, it prevents melting snow from soaking into the ground.

Colville River and other waterways in the region thaw for only about 10 weeks every summer.

Alaska's climate is as varied as its landscape. Along the southern coasts and islands, the weather is mild and very wet. Every year, Port Walter on the Alaska Panhandle receives about 220 inches (559 centimeters) of rain and melted snow—more than anywhere else in the United States!

Farther inland, away from the coast, the climate is dry and the winters are long and very cold. About 13 inches (33 cm) of moisture fall yearly. Winter temperatures can drop as low as –70° F (–57° C). But during the short summers, temperatures sometimes rise above 90° F (32° C).

Some parts of Alaska receive lots of snow.

Frost-covered red leaves add color to Alaska during the long cold season.

A hiker *(right)* **enjoys an overgrown trail in one of Alaska's many national parks.**

Along the Arctic coast, even the summers are cool. The average July temperature in this part of the state is only 47° F (8° C). Just 8 inches (20 cm) of **precipitation** fall here each year.

Summer on the Arctic Coastal Plain brings a brief display of hot-pink fireweed, blue forget-me-nots, and many other kinds of wildflowers. There are no trees on the coastal plain, but the state's other regions are heavily forested. Birch, western hemlock, Sitka spruce, and white spruce trees all grow in Alaska.

Alaska's Story

Across the Bering Strait, just 51 miles (82 kilometers) from Alaska, lies a part of Russia called Siberia. Long ago, a bridge of dry land crossed the Bering Strait, linking Siberia to what is now Alaska. During that time, between 10,000 and 40,000 years ago, many groups of people left Siberia in search of game and crossed the land bridge to Alaska. Descendants of these people are called Native Americans, or American Indians.

Some of the travelers passed through what is now Alaska and continued southward into present-day Canada and the Lower 48. Others stayed in the Alaska area. Two of Alaska's Indian groups, the Haidas and the Tlingits, settled on the coast of the Alaska Panhandle.

In front of their houses, the Indians raised huge, carved tree trunks called totem poles. As tall as telephone poles, the giant posts were carved with **totems**—images of plants and animals, such as frogs, ravens, and bears. Totems were believed to have magical powers.

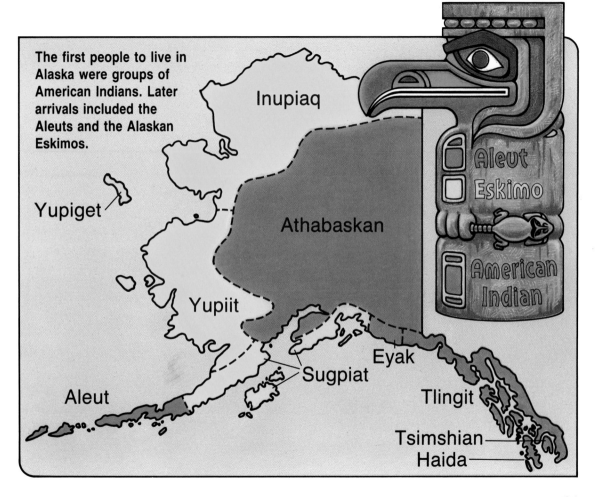

The first people to live in Alaska were groups of American Indians. Later arrivals included the Aleuts and the Alaskan Eskimos.

Inupiaq

Yupiget

Athabaskan

Yupiit

Eyak

Sugpiat

Aleut

Tlingit

Tsimshian

Haida

Aleut
Eskimo
American Indian

 otems

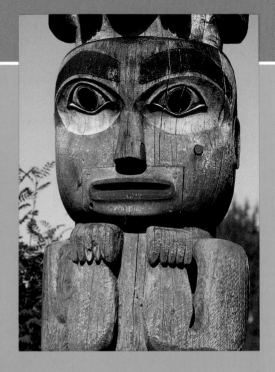

The Haidas and the Tlingits believed that certain animals had special powers. To represent these magical animals the Indians made images called totems. The totems were linked to privileges, or rights, that were claimed by families or individuals. A totem might stand for the right to use a special name, to perform a dance during a ceremony, or to wear a particular mask.

Families displayed their totems in many ways, using them to decorate almost everything they owned. Some wove totems into blankets and clothing or painted them on boxes. Others carved the totems into spear and knife handles or made masks with totems. But the most well-known display of the images was the totem pole. Some totem poles illustrated a family's history or honored a dead family member. Others celebrated a special event. Totem poles with openings carved through them often served as entrances to homes. No matter how totems were displayed, they were always symbols of power.

Scientists found these harpoon heads buried in ancient Eskimo graves near the Bering Strait.

The Athabaskans, another group of Indians, traveled in small bands throughout what is now the central part of Alaska. During the short summers, the Athabaskans gathered berries and caught fish. In the winter, they strapped snowshoes onto their feet to make walking over deep snow easier. The Athabaskans hunted caribou, moose, and mountain sheep with snares or bows and arrows, or by cornering the animals in corrals.

Thousands of years after the Indians arrived, groups now called the Alaskan Eskimos and the Aleuts arrived. These people made the journey from Siberia by boat, after the sea had covered the land bridge. The Alaskan Eskimos and the Aleuts settled mainly in coastal areas, hunting sea mammals for food and clothing.

From narrow boats called **kayaks,** the hunters harpooned seals, walrus, sea lions, and sea otters. Oiled seal or walrus skins were stretched over the boat's driftwood frame to keep cold water from slopping into the hunter's lap. Each hunter sat in the cockpit—a hole cut into the deck of each boat.

Unlike the Eskimos in what is now northern Canada, Alaskan Eskimos and Aleuts did not live in igloos, or houses made of snow and ice. Instead, they built homes with stones, driftwood, whale ribs, and blocks of earth and grass called sod. The dried intestines of sea mammals were stretched over the

Aleut hunters skimmed through rough waters in one-person boats called kayaks.

windows to keep out the cold and to let in sunlight.

Until the 1700s, Europeans had never met the Alaskan Eskimos and Aleuts or any of the American Indians in what is now Alaska. In 1725 Peter the Great, the czar (ruler) of Russia, decided to find out if any part of Siberia was connected to North America. The czar asked Vitus Bering, a Danish seaman, to travel by land to Siberia so he could set sail from the region's northeastern coast. In 1741, on their second journey, Bering and his crew found Alaska and proved that water completely separated North America from Siberia.

Bering's sailors returned to Russia with the pelts of sea otters, seals, and foxes—animals they had killed on the islands they visited. Siberian fur traders, eager to find new hunting grounds, headed for the region to collect furs.

Vitus Bering became the first European explorer to visit what is now Alaska.

25

Fur traders, able to earn huge profits selling pelts, soon swarmed over the Aleutian Islands, killing animals that the Aleuts depended on for food and clothing. The fur traders also stole furs from the Aleuts. Because the Aleuts were so skilled at hunting and boat building, the fur traders forced Aleut men to hunt animals for them, while they held Aleut women and children hostage.

In 1784 a fur trader named Grigory Shelekhov established the first Russian settlement in North America, on Kodiak Island. From this settlement, Shelekhov thought he could control the fur trade in the area, which became known as Russian America.

To keep warm, Aleuts wore long coats and dresses made of furs and skins.

Shelekhov's plan worked. In 1799 the Russian government gave complete control of the Russian American fur trade to Shelekhov's

Russian-American Company. Under the direction of Aleksandr Baranov, the Russian-American Company moved its headquarters to Sitka, on the Alaska Panhandle. Baranov took this land from the Tlingit Indians.

Angry, the Tlingits burned the Russian company's fort in 1802, killing most of the men and capturing the women and children. Two years later, the Russians attacked a Tlingit village near Sitka. The Tlingits fled but continued to attack Russian settlements for several years.

The town of Sitka served as Russian America's capital from 1807 to 1867.

Although the Russian-American Company maintained several settlements, only about 800 Russians ever lived in Russian America. And by the 1860s, the Russian fur traders had killed so many sea otters and other fur-bearing mammals that the animals were becoming harder and harder to find. Russia decided to sell the land they called Russian America.

The Russian government had never bought the land from the Alaskan Eskimos, Aleuts, or Indians. But in 1867, Russia signed a **treaty** with the United States, selling Russian America for just over $7 million, or about 2 cents per acre. The United States called the new land Alaska, after the Aleut name for the area—*Alyeska,* sometimes translated as "great land" or "main land."

Because the few residents of Alaska lived so far from each other, the area earned the nickname the Last Frontier. The name meant it was an unknown and

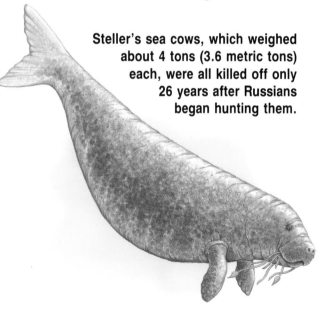

Steller's sea cows, which weighed about 4 tons (3.6 metric tons) each, were all killed off only 26 years after Russians began hunting them.

unsettled land. Alaska's vast wilderness would take years to explore, so it remained a true **frontier** for many decades.

In the first years that Alaska was part of the United States, churches sent **missionaries** to the Last Frontier. The missionaries wanted to teach the area's native people about the Christian religion and about the ways of life in the United States.

Forced to live in missionary villages, the native people attended mission churches and schools. Besides the Christian religion, children learned English, mathematics, reading, sewing, gardening, and carpentry. They were also encouraged to forget their old ways of life and their spiritual beliefs.

During a ceremony in 1867, officials lowered the Russian flag in Sitka and raised the U.S. flag in its place.

29

The arrival of white settlers changed many aspects of native culture. The newcomers, for example, encouraged native peoples to adopt different clothing *(left)*. Settlers and hunters killed so many whales and walrus that Eskimos began raising reindeer for meat *(facing page)*.

Like the Russian fur traders, many Americans saw Alaska as a place to make money. Companies from the Lower 48 liked working in Alaska because the local govern-ment didn't collect taxes or try to control businesses.

One industry that grew quickly was fish canning. Alaska's first cannery was built in 1878. In 1890 the operations along just one river on Kodiak Island processed three million salmon. By 1898 Alaska's coast was home to more than 55 canneries. They made huge profits selling the fish to the Lower 48 and to other countries.

As the canneries processed more fish, some Alaskans worried that salmon and other fish would be killed off completely. But the canneries were powerful. They were able to prevent the U.S. government from passing laws to control how many fish were taken from Alaska's rivers and ocean waters.

Other people were more interested in gold than fish. In 1896 prospectors George Washington Carmack, Skookum Jim Mason, and Tagish Charley found gold in Bonanza Creek. Right across the border from Alaska, the creek ran into Canada's Klondike River.

The Klondike discovery excited people from all over the United States. The easiest way to reach the Klondike region was to travel by ship to Alaska and then to cross the mountains following overland trails. At least 100,000 people headed through Alaska for the Klondike, hoping to become rich by finding their own nuggets of gold. During the cold winters, many of the gold seekers were killed by freezing temperatures. Avalanches in the mountains of

Alaska's newcomers, eager to find gold, dared to cross rough terrain in the mountains on their journey to the Klondike.

Alaska and of the Klondike region took the lives of other prospectors.

The gold in the Klondike encouraged prospectors to look for gold in Alaska, too. A few prospectors found the precious metal on the beaches of the Bering Sea in 1899. A shovel was all that was needed to scoop the gold out of the sand.

The town of Nome sprang up overnight as gold seekers rushed to the area. By 1900 Nome's population had climbed to 17,000, but most of the gold within easy reach had already been dug up. Only large mining companies with big, expensive equipment could continue to mine the area. Some of the town's residents opened stores, hotels, and other businesses to make a living.

In 1906 the U.S. government allowed Alaskans to elect a delegate, or nonvoting congressperson, to represent them in the nation's capital. Six years later, Alaska became an official U.S. territory. Many residents of the Last Frontier wanted the territory to become a state. The canneries and mining companies were against statehood. They feared the state government would pass laws that would limit their business activities.

By the early 1930s, only about 65,000 people were living in Alaska. Very few roads crossed the territory, and no roads connected Alaska to Canada or to the Lower 48. People and supplies traveled to and from the territory mostly by ship.

Matanuska's Miracle

In the 1930s, the U.S. economy was in poor shape. Many men and women had lost their jobs or their farms. To deal with some of these problems—and to help Alaska's population grow—the U.S. government came up with a plan in 1935. The government offered to move about 200 hard-hit, midwestern farm families to Alaska's Matanuska Valley.

The new settlers had no idea what to expect in the Last Frontier. High prices, no running water, and few tools made life difficult. Weeks of rainfall left the soil muddy and hard to work. Half of the newcomers gave up within three years. Although other families replaced those who quit, the settlers continued to struggle in the 1940s. By 1950 the experiment was finally working, and 60 percent of Alaska's farm products now come from the Matanuska Valley.

During World War II (1939–1945), the U.S. government built a highway to connect Alaska to the northernmost highways in Canada. Called the Alaska Highway, the road runs 1,397 miles (2,248 km) from Delta Junction, Alaska, to Dawson Creek, British Columbia. About 9,000 soldiers and 12,000 other workers built the road in less than a year.

The war itself came to Alaska, too. In June 1942, the Japanese bombed Dutch Harbor, a military base on the Aleutian Islands, and occupied two of the Aleutian Islands—Attu and Kiska. A year later, U.S. troops drove the Japanese off Attu. When Canadian and U.S. soldiers landed on Kiska Island later that summer, they

found only two dogs. The Japanese had already retreated.

A lot of the soldiers and construction workers who came to Alaska during the war stayed. By the end of the war, Alaska's population had grown to 112,000. Many of the territory's residents continued to call for statehood for Alaska. On January 3, 1959, Alaska became the 49th state and the first new state since 1912.

A Botched Evacuation

The United States became involved in World War II in December 1941, when the Japanese bombed Hawaii. By 1942 the Japanese had taken aim at bases in Alaska, too. In fact, the westernmost Aleutian island, Attu, was located only 600 miles (966 km) from Japanese soil.

In June 1942, the Japanese attacked Attu and captured its Aleut population. To protect the remaining Aleuts, the U.S. government decided to evacuate (remove) them by force. The more than 800 evacuees had little time to collect their belongings before being sent to camps in southeastern Alaska.

Conditions in the camps were terrible. The buildings could not keep out the cold, and there were not enough toilets, beds, and medical supplies. Many older Aleuts died during the wartime evacuation.

After the war ended in 1945, the Aleuts were allowed to return home. They usually found their belongings gone and their houses in ruins. In 1988 the U.S. government admitted that it had botched the evacuation. It offered the surviving Aleut evacuees an official apology and $12,000 each in damages.

In the years following statehood, Alaska saw a steady increase in its population. The growing population brought many changes to Alaska's wilderness and to the lives of its native people. Many newcomers began to clear and to build on the state's richest wilderness areas. As more new residents settled in the Last Frontier, the

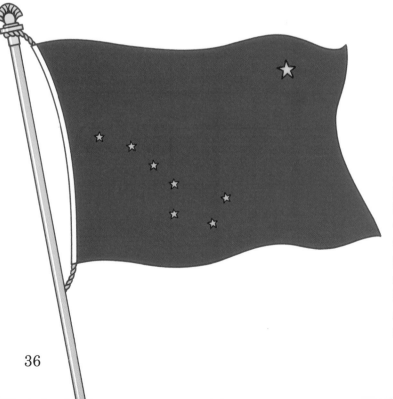

Alaska's state flag was designed by a 13-year-old Alaskan named Benny Benson. The flag features the Big Dipper and the North Star—famous stars that can be seen in the skies above Alaska. The blue background stands for the Alaskan sky and for the forget-me-not, Alaska's state flower.

For hundreds of years, Eskimos have lived in homes made of sod. Whale ribs support the walls and roofs.

area's native people were pushed off more and more of their traditional homelands.

After losing much of the land they had depended on for hunting and fishing, the native people were left with few ways to provide food, clothing, and shelter for themselves and their families. Many of the native people lived in remote areas of the state where there were few jobs, schools, or doctors' offices. Most had little money, and many were in poor health.

In 1971 the U.S. government returned 44 million acres (18 million hectares) of land to the Alaskan Eskimos, Aleuts, and American Indians. The native people set up special organizations called corporations to manage the land. They spent the money they earned on health care, on schools, and to create new jobs.

Some native people in Alaska still hunt and fish in traditional ways. Salmon, sometimes caught using fish wheel traps *(below),* are dried on racks *(right)* in the sun. Hunters often store animal pelts *(lower right)* in buildings on stilts.

In 1980 the U.S. government set aside more than 100 million acres (40 million ha) of land in the Last Frontier for national parks, forests, and wilderness areas. That same year, the government also gave special hunting and fishing rights to native people in these areas.

Questions about preserving Alaska's wilderness arose when oil was discovered at Prudhoe Bay on the Arctic coast. The Trans-Alaska pipeline was built for transporting the oil from Prudhoe Bay to the port at Valdez on Alaska's southern coast. From here, the oil is shipped to the Lower 48.

The pipeline has provided many jobs for Alaskans and has been a big boost to the economy. But some people feared that oil companies would spill oil while drilling for it or transporting it.

In 1989 Alaskans' fears about oil pollution came true. An oil tanker named the *Exxon Valdez* ran aground near Valdez and spilled more than 10 million gallons (38 million liters) of oil into Prince William Sound, an ocean inlet off the state's southern coast. The oil contaminated large parts of Alaska's coastline and killed hundreds of thousands of birds, fish, and other animals.

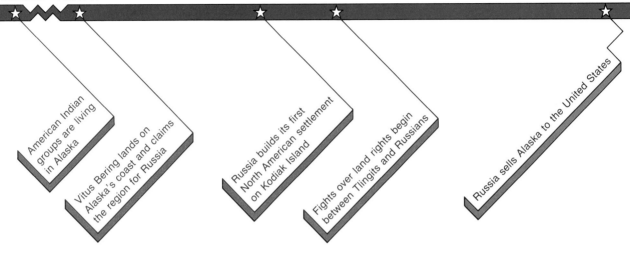

8000 B.C.   A.D. 1741   1784   1802   1867

American Indian groups are living in Alaska

Vitus Bering lands on Alaska's coast and claims the region for Russia

Russia builds its first North American settlement on Kodiak Island

Fights over land rights begin between Tlingits and Russians

Russia sells Alaska to the United States

The Trans-Alaska pipeline, which crosses 800 miles (1,287 km), was built in a zigzag pattern.

40

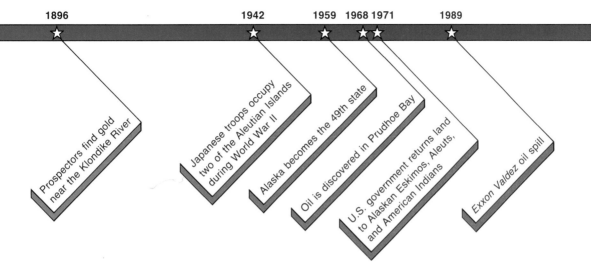

1896 Prospectors find gold near the Klondike River

1942 Japanese troops occupy two of the Aleutian Islands during World War II

1959 Alaska becomes the 49th state

1968 Oil is discovered in Prudhoe Bay

1971 U.S. government returns land to Alaskan Eskimos, Aleuts, and American Indians

1989 *Exxon Valdez* oil spill

The 49th state faces difficult decisions in the years to come. Alaskans hope to find a way to keep mining and fishing jobs and still preserve the state's wildlife and natural beauty. In this way, the state can continue to live up to its nickname—the Last Frontier.

41

Living and Working in Alaska

In some parts of Alaska, mail is delivered by airplane. That's because many small towns have no roads connecting them to the outside world. With so few people living in vast areas of the state, Alaska can't afford to keep up many roads. The Last Frontier counts less than one person for every square mile (2.6 sq. km).

Signs *(above)* show the long distances that Alaskans have to travel from one city to another. Wooden houses *(facing page)* line a street in Ketchikan, a seaport in southeastern Alaska.

But most Alaskans do have neighbors—and roads connecting them. About two-thirds of the state's 552,000 residents live in or near cities. Alaska's largest city, Anchorage, is home to about one-third of the state's population. Next in size is Fairbanks, with 70,000 people in the city and surrounding area, and then Juneau—the state capital—with about 27,000 people.

Anchorage is located in southern Alaska. An earthquake in 1964 badly damaged the city, which has since been rebuilt.

Alaska's young people find lots to do outdoors.

Native people make up about 13 percent of Alaska's total population. The largest number of these native people are Alaskan Eskimos. Many of the 13,000 Inupiat live in the northern and western parts of the state. About 24,000 Yupiit, Yupiget, and Sugpiat make their homes in the Pacific Mountains, on Saint Lawrence Island, and on Kodiak Island.

The Aleutian Islands and the Alaska Peninsula are home to many of the 8,000 Aleuts in Alaska. More than 24,000 Haidas, Tlingits, Athabaskans, Tsimshians, and other American Indians also live in different parts of the state.

A fisher checks his crab trap.

Most of Alaska's non-native residents have European ancestors. Many of them moved north to the state from the Lower 48, and others arrived with the U.S. military. Some Alaskans came directly from Europe. Many of the residents of Petersburg, for example, are descendants of Norwegian fishers.

People in towns like Petersburg depend on the ocean to earn a living. Many Alaskans who live near the coast fish for salmon, crabs, halibut, herring, and shrimp.

Mining makes the largest amount of money for Alaska, and 95 percent of these earnings come from oil. Many companies drill for oil at Prudhoe Bay, one of the most active oil-producing regions in the world.

Mining companies also search for gold near Nome and Fairbanks. A large deposit of molybdenum, a metal used in making steel, is mined near Ketchikan. Alaskans dig up sand, gravel, and crushed stone to build roads. Coal, lead, silver, tin, zinc, and natural gas are also mined in Alaska.

Many of Alaska's manufacturing jobs are tied to the state's mining and fishing industries. Alaskans work in canneries that clean and package the salmon, crab, herring, and other fish caught in Alaskan waters. Other people work in oil refineries, where oil is processed to make petroleum products such as gasoline and plastic. Some Alaskans make paper and wood products from Alaska's timber.

Alaska's sawmills and pulp mills make a variety of wood and paper products.

Guides dressed in traditional Russian clothing lead tours of Sitka.

The service industry employs the most Alaskans. A lot of service workers assist the tourists that visit the state. Other service workers teach in Alaska's schools or treat patients in the state's hospitals. Others have jobs as lawyers, police officers, salespeople, and news reporters.

A few Alaskans farm, especially in the fertile Matanuska Valley of central Alaska. On the state's 650 farms, Alaskans raise beef and dairy cattle, chickens, pigs, and sheep. Some Alaskan Eskimos raise reindeer for meat. Farmers also grow grains, fruits, and vegetables, such as wheat, cabbages, and potatoes.

The fur industry still provides jobs for some Alaskans. But most hunters no longer search for fur-bearing animals at sea. Instead, Alaskans trap land animals, including wolves, beavers, wolverines, lynx, marten, and mink.

Most of the roads in Alaska link cities such as Anchorage and Fairbanks to the Alaska Highway. Travelers also can catch one of the ferries that chug up and down Alaska's coastline, stopping at cities and towns on the Alaska Panhandle and along the state's southern coast. The Alaska Railroad carries people and supplies from the port at Seward to Anchorage and Fairbanks.

The Alaska Railroad follows a scenic route along the coast, over mountains, and through deep forests.

People traveling to and from Alaska's wilderness areas often rely on small planes called air taxis.

Alaska's airports, ferries, and roads bring about 800,000 tourists to Alaska each year. Visitors have plenty to see and do. For example, they can learn about Alaska's history, its people, and its land at the state's museums.

In Sitka the Sheldon Jackson Museum—the oldest museum in the state—displays kayaks, dog-sleds, masks, and other useful items made by Alaska's native people. Exhibits at the Alaska State Museum in Juneau feature everything from Russian culture in Alaska to wildlife and modern art. At the University of Alaska Museum in Fairbanks, displays describe how gold and copper are mined, and visitors can see a 3-ton (2.7-metric ton) copper nugget.

One of Alaska's most exciting sports is dog mushing, or sled-dog racing. Every March dog teams compete in the Iditarod Trail Sled Dog Race, which covers a grueling 1,049-mile (1,688-km) route from Anchorage to Nome.

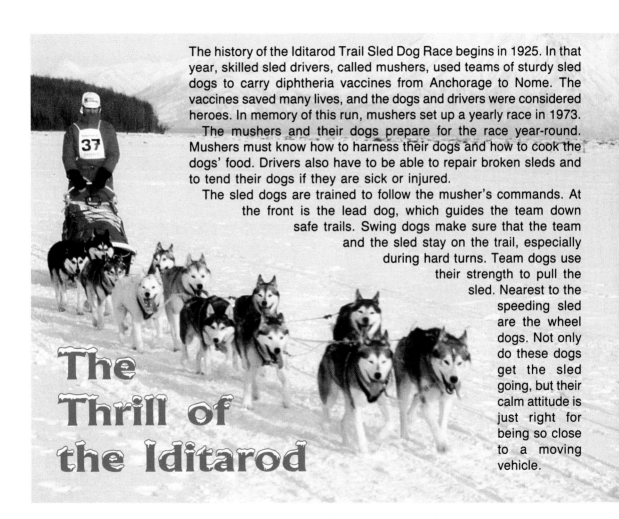

The history of the Iditarod Trail Sled Dog Race begins in 1925. In that year, skilled sled drivers, called mushers, used teams of sturdy sled dogs to carry diphtheria vaccines from Anchorage to Nome. The vaccines saved many lives, and the dogs and drivers were considered heroes. In memory of this run, mushers set up a yearly race in 1973.

The mushers and their dogs prepare for the race year-round. Mushers must know how to harness their dogs and how to cook the dogs' food. Drivers also have to be able to repair broken sleds and to tend their dogs if they are sick or injured.

The sled dogs are trained to follow the musher's commands. At the front is the lead dog, which guides the team down safe trails. Swing dogs make sure that the team and the sled stay on the trail, especially during hard turns. Team dogs use their strength to pull the sled. Nearest to the speeding sled are the wheel dogs. Not only do these dogs get the sled going, but their calm attitude is just right for being so close to a moving vehicle.

The Thrill of the Iditarod

Thousands of skiers, hikers, and climbers visit Alaska's wilderness areas each year. Skiers can whoosh down the slopes just outside downtown Anchorage. Or they can go by helicopter to the Juneau Ice Field and trek down one of Alaska's glaciers.

Daring sports enthusiasts in Alaska try everything from ice climbing (above) **to white-water kayaking** (right).

Hikers can follow the Chilkoot Trail—the old route of the Klondike gold prospectors—at Klondike Gold Rush National Historical Park near Skagway. Visitors may spot moose or Dall sheep wandering across the hiking trails of Alaska's many parks. Experienced climbers can try to reach the top of Mount McKinley in Denali National Park.

For people who enjoy water sports, Alaska's rivers offer the thrill of white-water canoeing, kayaking, and rafting. Anglers fish for trout and salmon. But anglers have to share their favorite fishing spots—salmon are also one of the favorite foods of bald eagles and grizzly bears!

An angler snags an unexpected catch—a giant octopus!

Protecting the Environment

When the *Exxon Valdez* oil tanker ran aground in Prince William Sound in March 1989, 11 million gallons (42 million l) of oil gushed from the ship's hull, or body, where the oil was stored. The oil, drilled at Prudhoe Bay and carried by the Trans-Alaska pipeline to Valdez, was on its way to the Lower 48.

The oil spread across 3,000 square miles (7,770 sq km) of ocean and washed up on more than 1,500 miles (2,414 km) of beach along the Alaskan coast. After the spill, seabirds thought the dark patches of oil were schools of fish. The birds plunged through the oil to catch fish, and the oil coated their feathers, gluing them together. Without clean, fluffed feathers, the birds couldn't keep themselves warm in the ice-cold ocean waters.

After the *Exxon Valdez* *(below)* got stuck on an underwater reef, another ship anchored beside it to help remove the oil. But most of the oil spilled into the surrounding water and washed up onto land *(left)*.

Many oiled birds died from exposure to the cold. Others were poisoned by the oil—either by swallowing it as they tried to clean their feathers or by eating oil-contaminated fish. Some birds died when the oil soaked through their skin.

A wildlife biologist holds up a dead bald eagle coated with oil *(left),* **while a member of a cleanup crew examines the body of an oiled sea otter** *(above).*

Scientists estimate that between 375,000 and 580,000 seabirds died. As many as 7,200 sea otters may have died, too, along with whales, bald eagles, salmon, and other animals and plants.

The Exxon Corporation was held responsible for cleaning up the oil. The cleanup crews tried several methods. Workers used **booms**, which look like big, floating logs, to surround the oil and keep it from spreading. Boats called **skimmers** were equipped with vacuums to suck up the oil trapped by the booms.

The cleanup crews also tried using **dispersants**—chemicals that break up an oil slick into small droplets of oil. The droplets then disperse, or spread out, in the water, speeding up the natural decaying process of the oil. Dispersants help thin out oil slicks faster, but they also mix oil into the surrounding water, making it poisonous for fish.

Booms surround a contaminated coastal area, where cleanup crews work to remove the oil.

Using straw and heavy-duty paper towels, workers clean rocks on the beach.

Along the beaches, workers used peat moss, straw, and chemicals to soak up the oil. Workers also sprayed powerful jets of hot water to force the oil back into the water, where it could be picked up by skimmers. But this hot-water method killed marine creatures that could not survive in the high water temperatures. The water jets pushed oil under the sand and rocks and even deeper into the ground.

Another method tested by scientists from the Environmental Protection Agency (EPA) was to speed the growth of certain oil-eating bacteria on the beaches. The bacteria needed additional nutrients to be able to use the oil as food. So the EPA sprayed nutrient-rich fertilizer on the bacteria, causing them to grow and eat more and more of the oil.

After many months of cleaning up the oil, researchers and cleanup crews still couldn't tell how successful their efforts had been. Years may pass before Alaskans know what long-term effects the oil spill will have on their environment.

People generally agree that the best way to protect Alaska's wild-life, beaches, and water from oil pollution is to stop oil from spilling in the first place. By using extra care in transporting oil, the operators of oil tankers can avoid oil leaks. To help prevent oil spills, some people want oil to be carried in ships that are built with two hulls—an inner one for oil storage and an outer one for protection. That way, if a tanker runs aground, only the outer hull is likely to crack, leaving the inner hull and the oil untouched.

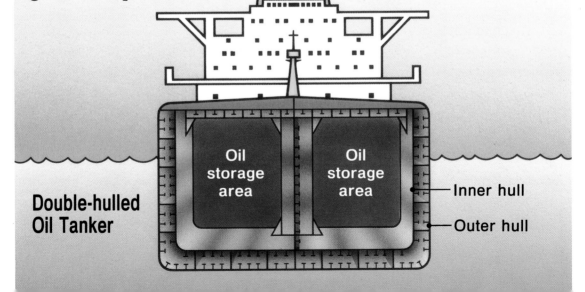

Double-hulled Oil Tanker

Oil storage area

Oil storage area

Inner hull

Outer hull

Because millions of people depend on oil to heat their homes and fuel their cars, oil companies will probably not stop drilling for or transporting oil. But some people want oil exploration in Alaska to end. In particular, they don't want oil companies to drill in the Arctic National Wildlife Refuge on Alaska's northern coast. Oil companies want to drill in the refuge because they suspect it has vast amounts of oil hidden beneath the permafrost.

People in favor of leaving the refuge alone are afraid that drill-

The grasses of the Arctic National Wildlife Refuge feed a variety of animals.

ing will threaten the animals and the people who live there. The refuge is home to large caribou herds and to 200 other kinds of Arctic animals, such as polar bears and musk-ox. Some native people in the area rely on the caribou for food and clothing.

People who want oil companies to drill in the wildlife refuge argue that oil is important to Alaska's economy. Since oil was discovered at Prudhoe Bay in 1968, the oil industry has provided thousands of jobs for Alaskans. Money raised by taxing oil companies is used to pay many government workers. The state's oil profits have allowed Alaska to stop collecting income taxes and to pay residents part of the money it earns from oil.

Oil from Prudhoe Bay will eventually run out. For this reason, many Alaskans want the jobs and money that drilling in the Arctic National Wildlife Refuge could bring. But if oil is found and drilled for in the refuge, it will likely run out someday, too. So sooner or later Alaskans will have to find another way to earn money.

The U.S. government controls the Arctic National Wildlife Refuge and other wilderness areas in the state. Alaskans and other U.S. citizens can let the government know how they feel about drilling for oil in Alaska. Together, the people will decide if the risks to the environment are worth the oil, jobs, and money that come from drilling in the Last Frontier.

Alaska's Famous People

ACTIVISTS

Celia M. Hunter (born 1919) ferried military planes to U.S. bases during World War II. After moving to Alaska, she set up a wilderness camp and became active in efforts to protect Alaska's environment. In 1976 Hunter became president of The Wilderness Society, a national environmental organization.

Howard Rock (1911–1976), born in Point Hope, Alaska, was a successful artist before founding the *Tundra Times* in 1962. The Anchorage-based newspaper voiced the concerns of Alaskan Eskimos and American Indians and helped to file the first legal suits supporting native land claims.

Hudson Stuck (1863–1920) led the 1913 expedition that was the first to reach the tallest peak of Mount McKinley. He was more famous as an Episcopalian missionary who fought to preserve the ways of Alaska's native people.

CELIA HUNTER ▶

◀ HOWARD ROCK

◀ HUDSON STUCK

ADVENTURERS

Vitus Bering (1681–1741), a Danish-born navigator who worked for Russia, landed on the Alaskan coast in 1741. His explorations proved that water separated Asia and North America. Bering Sea, Bering Strait, and Bering Island are named after him.

62

JOSEPH JUNEAU ▶

Joseph Juneau (1826–1900), while in his fifties, discovered gold in Alaska's first major gold strike. According to tradition, Juneau cried when he found the valuable metal, either in joy or in sorrow at being too old to spend his riches. The capital city of Juneau is named after him.

SYDNEY LAURENCE ▼

ARTISTS

Sydney M. Laurence (1865–1940), although born in New York, visited Alaska frequently throughout his later life and died in Anchorage. His paintings, which captured the beauty of the Alaskan wilderness, often featured Mount McKinley.

Virgil Partch (1916–1984), a cartoonist, was born on Saint Paul Island, Alaska. After being fired by the Disney studios for participating in a strike, Partch began to sell his cartoons to newspapers and magazines, including *Newsweek* and *Time*. His famous signature, VIP, appeared on all his drawings.

DONALD ▲ SIMPSON

ENTERTAINMENT FIGURES

Victor Jory (1902–1982), born in Dawson City, Alaska, was an actor who became famous for his "bad guy" roles. He appeared in many films and television shows, including *The Adventures of Tom Sawyer, Gone with the Wind,* and "Ironside."

◀ VICTOR JORY

Donald Simpson (born 1945) is a film producer whose hit movies include *Flashdance, Top Gun,* and *Beverly Hills Cop.* The son of a hunting guide, Simpson was born in Anchorage.

63

INVENTOR

Leroy Parsons (1907–1989), the inventor of cable television, moved to Alaska in 1953 and by 1967 had installed the state's first cable system. The system, set up in Barrow, Alaska, allowed people living there to watch television for the first time.

POLITICAL LEADERS

Edward Lewis ("Bob") Bartlett (1904–1968) grew up in Fairbanks and became a gold miner, a journalist, and finally a U.S. senator. After fighting for Alaskan statehood, Bartlett championed the passage of health laws and was one of the first senators to oppose the Vietnam War.

Ernest Gruening (1887–1974), although trained as a doctor, became a journalist specializing in international affairs. In 1939 Gruening moved to Alaska to become territorial governor and worked hard for statehood. After Alaska became a state, he was elected to the U.S. Senate, where he campaigned for the rights of native people.

◄ **ERNEST GRUENING**

◄ **BOB BARTLETT**

Andrew Isaac (1898–1991) was chief of the United Crow Band for 59 years. Born in a trapping camp, Isaac honored the traditional ways of his people but also emphasized the value of education and helped to wage the war against drugs and alcohol among Alaska's native people.

SPORTS FIGURES

Susan Butcher (born 1954), a skilled dog musher and trainer living near Eureka, Alaska, is the first person ever to win three

◄ SUSAN BUTCHER

Iditarod races in a row—in 1986, 1987, and 1988. She won again in 1990. Her racing ability and her close relationship with her sled dogs have made her a tough competitor.

Dorothy Page (1921–1989) and **Joe Redington** (born 1917) organized the first Iditarod race in 1967 to mark the 100th anniversary of the sale of Alaska to the United States. That first run covered only part of the historic Iditarod trail blazed by mushers in 1925. By 1973, when the trail had been fully cleared, the race crossed more than 1,000 miles (1,690 km) and carried a prize of $50,000.

Mark Schlereth (born 1966), the first Alaskan-born athlete in the National Football League, has played guard for the Washington Redskins since 1989. A dedicated lineman from Anchorage, Schlereth is nicknamed "Stinky" after an Alaskan food made from rotting fishheads.

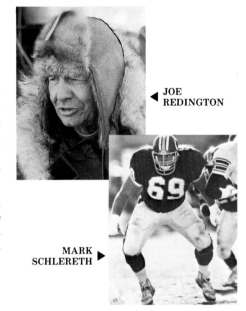

◀ JOE
REDINGTON

MARK ▶
SCHLERETH

◀ BETZI WOODMAN

WRITERS

Nora M. Dauenhauer (born 1927) spoke only Tlingit until she was eight years old and went to school. Her love of her native language has led her to collect, translate, and preserve the stories that Tlingits have long passed down by word of mouth.

Betzi M. Woodman (1913–1990), a daring news reporter for Reuters, gave the world its first eyewitness account of the severe earthquake that shook Alaska in 1964. Her prize-winning work took her to oil platforms, ice floes, and underground nuclear test sites.

65

Facts-at-a-Glance

Nickname: Last Frontier
Song: ''Alaska's Flag''
Motto: North to the Future
Flower: forget-me-not
Tree: Sitka spruce
Bird: willow ptarmigan

Population: 551,947*
Rank in population, nationwide: 49th
Area: 656,424 sq mi (1,700,138 sq km)
Rank in area, nationwide: 1st
Date and ranking of statehood:
   January 3, 1959, the 49th state
Capital: Juneau
Major cities (and populations*):
   Anchorage (226,338), Fairbanks (30,843),
   Juneau (26,751), Sitka (8,588), Ketchikan (8,263)
U.S. senators: 2
U.S. representatives: 1
Electoral votes: 3

Places to visit: Chilkat Bald Eagle Preserve near Haines, Alaska Zoo in Anchorage, Dog Mushing Museum in Fairbanks, Museum of History and Art in Anchorage, Valley of 10,000 Smokes in Katmai National Park and Preserve

Annual Events: Iditarod Trail Sled Dog Race (Feb. or March), Salmon Derby in Sitka (May), Midnight Sun Festival in Nome (June), World Eskimo-Indian Olympics in Fairbanks (July), Alaska State Fair in Palmer (Aug.)

* 1990 census

66

| Average January temperature: 5° F (–15° C) | Average July temperature: 55° F (13° C) |

Natural resources: oil, natural gas, gold, coal, zinc, molybdenum, tin, sand, gravel, fish and shellfish, forests, water

Agricultural products: milk, eggs, beef cattle, reindeer, grains, potatoes, greenhouse products

Manufactured goods: fish and seafood products, wood and paper products, construction materials

ENDANGERED AND THREATENED SPECIES
Mammals—humpback whale, right whale, blue whale, bowhead whale, gray whale, sperm whale, fin whale, sei whale, Steller's sea lion
Birds—bald eagle, Eskimo curlew, American peregrine falcon, Arctic peregrine falcon, short-tailed albatross, Aleutian Canada goose
Reptiles—green sea turtle, leatherneck sea turtle

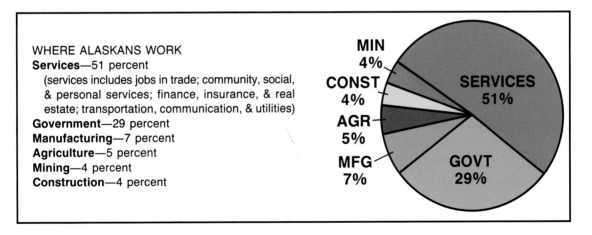

WHERE ALASKANS WORK
Services—51 percent
(services includes jobs in trade; community, social, & personal services; finance, insurance, & real estate; transportation, communication, & utilities)
Government—29 percent
Manufacturing—7 percent
Agriculture—5 percent
Mining—4 percent
Construction—4 percent

MIN
4%
CONST
4%
AGR
5%
MFG
7%
SERVICES
51%
GOVT
29%

Aleut (al-ee-OOT)

Bering, **Vitus** (BEHR-ihng, VEE-tuhs)

Denali (duh-NAH-lee)

Haida (HY-duh)

Iditarod (eye-DIHT-uh-rahd)

Inupiat (in-OO-pee-at)

Juneau (JOO-noh)

Prudhoe (PRUHD-hoh)

Sugpiat (SUHK-pat)

Tlingit (TLING-kuht)

Tsimshian (TSIM-shee-uhn)

Valdez (val-DEEZ)

Yupiget (yoo-PEE-khet)

Yupiit (yoo-PEET)

Glossary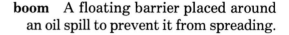

boom A floating barrier placed around an oil spill to prevent it from spreading.

dispersant An agent that helps one substance to disperse, or scatter, into another substance.

frontier A part of a settled country that lies next to a region that is still wilderness.

glacier A large body of ice and snow that moves slowly over land.

kayak A light Eskimo canoe that holds one person. The boat's wooden frame is covered with skins, except for a hole in the center for the kayaker.

missionary A person sent out by a religious group to spread its beliefs to other people.

peninsula   A stretch of land almost completely surrounded by water.

permafrost   Ground that remains frozen for two or more years. In Alaska, continuous permafrost occurs north of the Brooks Range and in high mountain regions.

precipitation   Rain, snow, and other forms of moisture that fall to earth.

skimmer   A boat equipped to pick up oil trapped by booms. Some skimmers have large ramps that scoop up the oil; others have large vacuum-like hoses that suck up the oil.

totem   An animal or other object from nature taken by a family or tribe as its symbol. The images of totems decorate poles called totem poles.

treaty   An agreement between two or more groups, usually having to do with peace or trade.

Index

Acknowledgments:

Maryland Cartographics, pp. 2, 10–11; Harold Wahlman, pp. 2–3, 17; Jack Lindstrom, p. 6; Mary Ney, p. 7; Hodgens' Photography, p. 8; NE Stock Photo: © Jim Schwabel, pp. 9, 52 (right), © Peter Cole, p. 13, © Grant Klotz, pp. 46, 47, 52 (left); Root Resources: © Alan G. Nelson, p. 10, © Kenneth W. Fink, p. 37, © Ruth Smith, p. 42; Lynn M. Stone, pp. 12, 15 (both), 49, 50; Visuals Unlimited: © Steve McCutcheon, pp. 14, 43, 44, © Will Troyer, pp. 55 (left), 69; Kent & Donna Dannen, p. 16; Jerry Hennen, pp. 18, 38 (bottom left & top right); © G. W. Biedel / Laatsch-Hupp Photo, p. 19; Betty Groskin, p. 22; IPS, pp. 23, 27, 32, 48; AK and Polar Regions Dept., Univ. of AK Fairbanks: Rare Book Coll. (acc. #60024), p. 24, Charles E. Bunnell Coll. (acc. #73-66-217N), p. 62 (bottom), Barrett Willoughby Coll. (acc. #72-116-413), p. 63 (center left), Klerekoper Coll. (acc. #77-158-178), p. 64 (top); AK State Library, Early Prints of AK Coll., p. 25; Library of Congress, pp. 26, 64 (center); Stock Montage, p. 29; Smithsonian Institution (photo #75-5355), p. 30; Glenbow Archives, Calgary, Alberta (neg. #NC1-890), p. 31; Brown Brothers, Sterling, PA, p. 34; AK at War Coll., Univ. of AK Anchorage, Archives & Manuscripts Dept., p. 35; Marge & Joe Skubic, p. 38 (bottom right); Adam Lerner, pp. 40, 71; John S. Foster, pp. 45, 65 (top); Nancy Budrow, p. 51; Paul Ashner, p. 53; Mike Lewis / ADEC; p. 55 (right); Bruce Batten, U.S. Fish and Wildlife Service, p. 56 (left); 3M / Occupational Health & Environmental Safety Div., p. 56 (right); Oil Spill Public Information Center, p. 57; Erich Gundlach / ADEC, p. 58; © Scott T. Smith, p. 60; Kathy Kilmer, p. 62 (top); *Tundra Times,* p. 62 (center); Dictionary of American Portraits, p. 63 (top); Hollywood Book & Poster, p. 63 (center right & bottom); © Susan Braine / Dembinsky Photo, p. 64 (bottom); Washington Redskins, p. 65 (center); Lyman L. Woodman, p. 65 (bottom); Jean Matheny, p. 66.